Feelings

Caring

Sarah Medina

Illustrated by Jo Brooker

Heinemann Library
Chicago, Illinois

Customer Service   888–454–2279
Visit our website at www.heinemannlibrary.com

Photo research by Erica Martin
Designed by Jo Malivoire
Printed in China by South China Printing Company Limited

11 10 09 08 07
10 9 8 7 6 5 4 3 2 1

Library of Congress Cataloging-in-Publication Data
Medina, Sarah, 1960-
 Caring / Sarah Medina.
   p. cm. -- (Feelings)
 Includes bibliographical references and index.
 ISBN-13: 978-1-4034-9295-1 (library binding-hardcover)
 ISBN-10: 1-4034-9295-6 (library binding-hardcover)
 ISBN-13: 978-1-4034-9302-6 (pbk.)
 ISBN-10: 1-4034-9302-2 (pbk.)
 1. Caring--Juvenile literature. I. Title.
 BJ1475.M43 2007
 177'.7--dc22
                              2006025216

Acknowledgments
The author and publisher are grateful to the following for permission to reproduce
copyright material: Bananastock p. **22A**, **B**, D; Getty Images/Taxi p. **22C**; Getty Images/
photodisc p. **6**, **7**.

Every effort has been made to contact copyright holders of any material reproduced
in this book. Any omissions will be rectified in subsequent printings if notice is given
to the publisher.

Contents

What Does Caring Mean? 4

What Happens When I Am Caring? 6

Why Should I Be Caring? 8

Is It Easy to Be Caring? 10

How Can I Be Caring? 12

Are People Always Caring? 14

Can I Help Someone to Be Caring? 16

What Should I Do When Someone Is Caring? 18

Enjoy Being Caring! 20

What Are These Feelings? 22

Picture Glossary 23

Index 24

Some words are shown in bold, **like this**. They are explained in the glossary on page 23.

What Does Caring Mean?

Caring is like a **feeling**. When you have different feelings, you do or say different things.

angry

proud

sad

When you are caring, you think of how others feel. You do nice things for people.

What Happens When I Am Caring?

When you are caring, you want to be kind to other people.

You think about how you can help them.

Why Should I Be Caring?

When you are caring, you make people feel happy. You make yourself feel good, too!

When you are caring, other people **notice**. This can show them how to be more caring, too.

Is It Easy to Be Caring?

Being caring is great, but it is not always easy! Sometimes you have to remember to be caring.

Think about how nice it feels when someone is caring. Then decide how you can be caring, too.

How Can I Be Caring?

You can be caring in lots of ways. You can help to make breakfast or clean the house.

You can remember to say, "Please"
and "Thank you." Try to say something
nice to someone every day.

Are People Always Caring?

Sometimes people forget to be caring. They might be too busy.

Be caring to them, anyway. Then they might remember that being caring is best!

Can I Help Someone to Be Caring?

You can show other people how to be caring. Think of ways you can be caring together.

If your baby brother is asleep, you can play quietly so you do not wake him up.

17

What Should I Do When Someone Is Caring?

When people are caring to you, tell them how great it feels. Say a big "Thank you!"

Do something nice for them another time. Then they will know that you care about them, too.

19

Enjoy Being Caring!

Being caring is wonderful! It makes other people feel good. It makes you feel great, too.

If someone is caring, be happy. Then pass on the good **feeling**. Be caring to someone else!

21

What Are These Feelings?

A

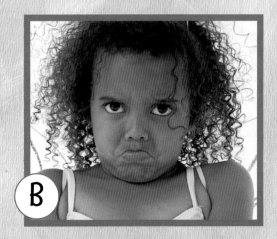

B

C

D

Which of these people look happy?
What are the other people feeling?

Look at page 24 to see the answers.

22

Picture Glossary

feeling
something that you feel
inside. Caring is like
a feeling.

notice
see; become aware of

Index

baby brother 17

breakfast 12

feelings 4, 21

house 13

Answers to the questions on page 22

The person in picture C looks happy. The other people could be sad, angry, or jealous.

Note to Parents and Teachers

Reading for information is an important part of a child's literacy development. Learning begins with a question about something. Help children think of themselves as investigators and researchers by encouraging their questions about the world around them. Most chapters in this book begin with a question. Read the question together. Look at the pictures. Talk about what you think the answer might be. Then read the text to find out if your predictions were correct. Think of other questions you could ask about the topic, and discuss where you might find the answers. Assist children in using the picture glossary and the index to practice new vocabulary and research skills.

24